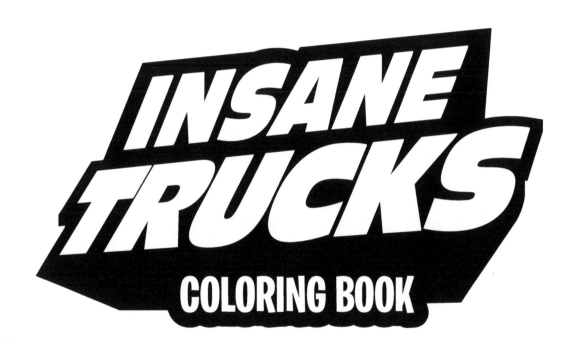

INSANE TRUCKS
COLORING BOOK

Check out heydanielvera.com for more products!
Share your work **#heydanielvera** on social media

AN AUTHOR'S NOTE FOR A FUTURE ARTIST

Thank you very much for purchasing my book!
I really value your support and hope you have a lot of fun.

I have dedicated half of my life to drawing, painting and designing cars.

One day it occurred to me to design the car coloring book that I dreamed
of having when I was your age, but for some reason, it didn't exist.
So I said: why not do it myself?

I hope you enjoy each piece of art in this book as much as I enjoyed making it,
so I look forward to seeing your finished masterpieces.

Please tag @heydanielvera or use #heydanielvera

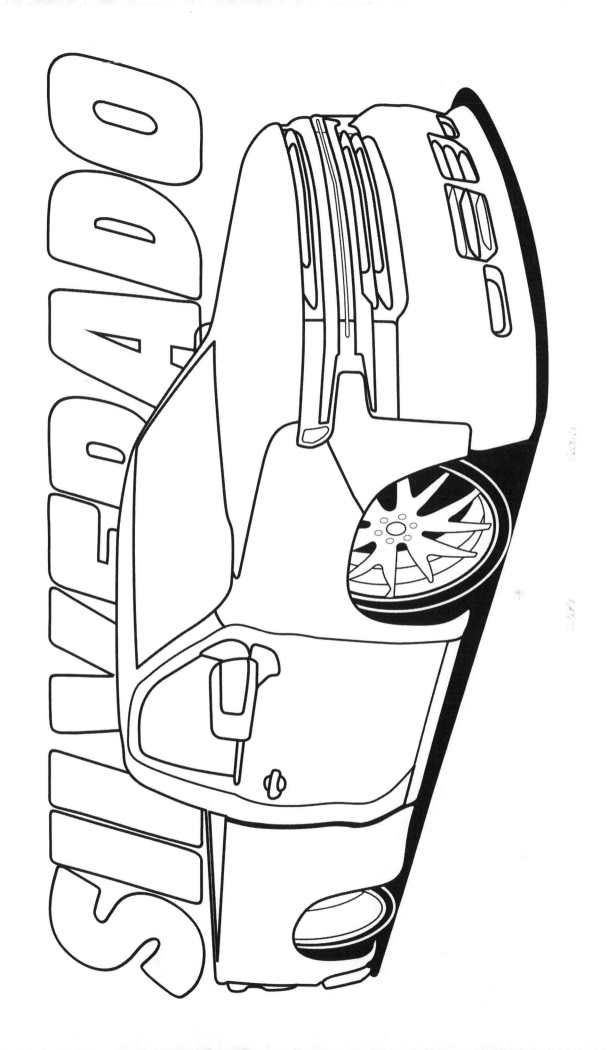

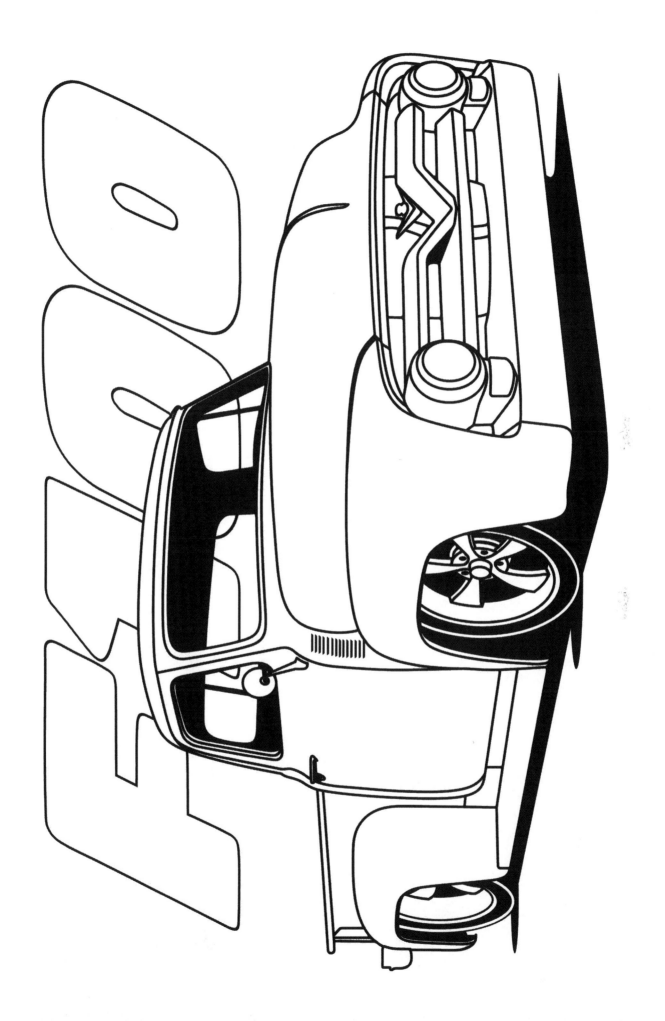

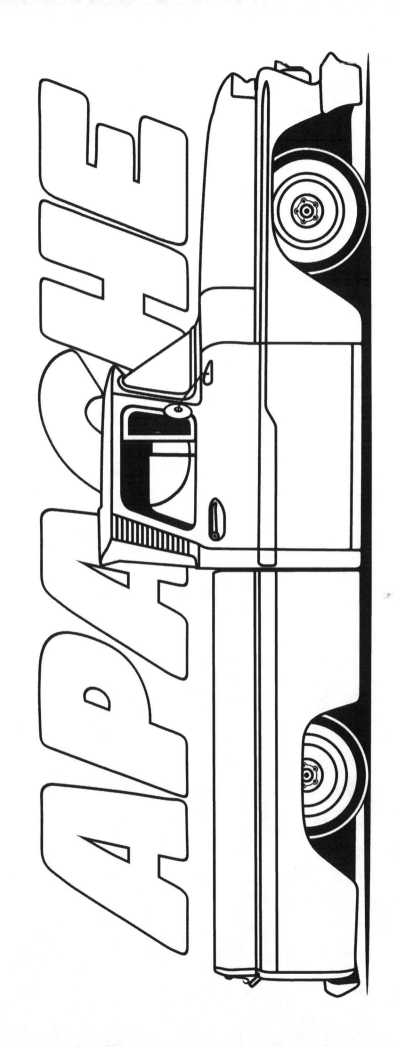

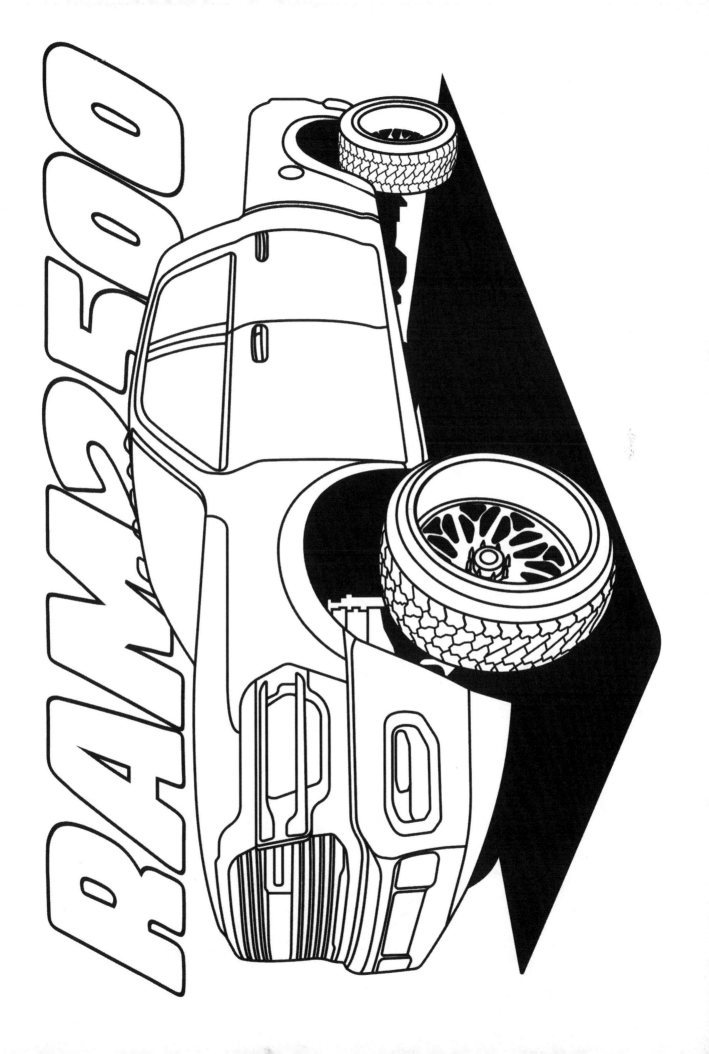

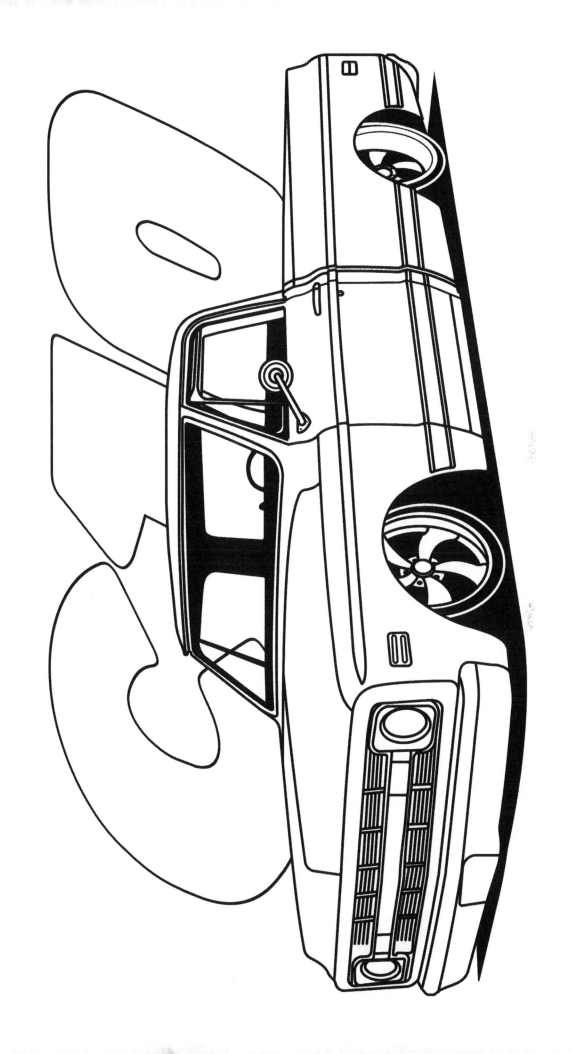

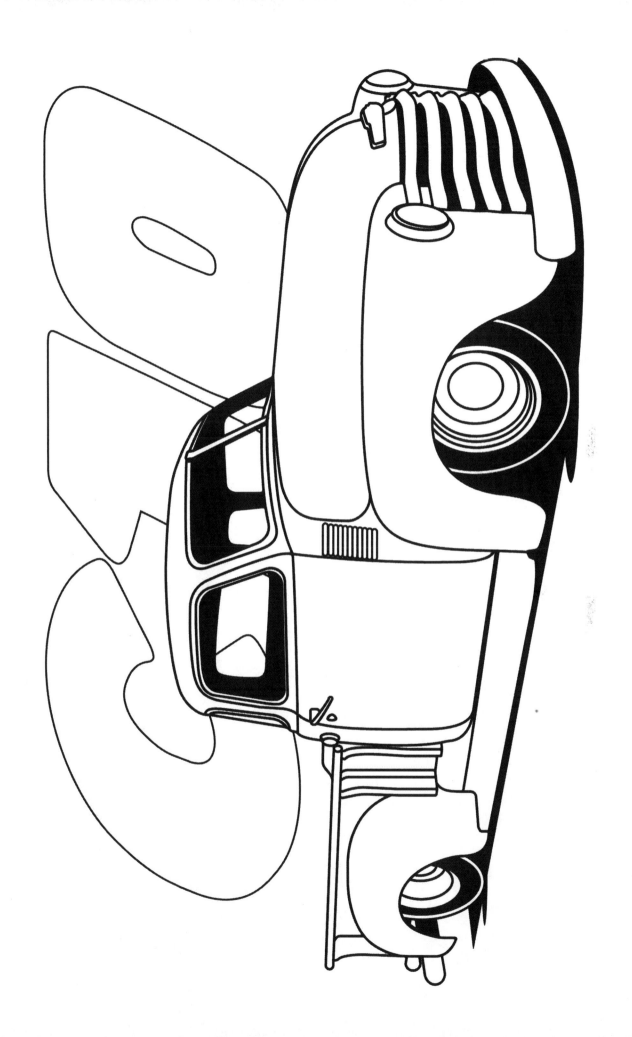

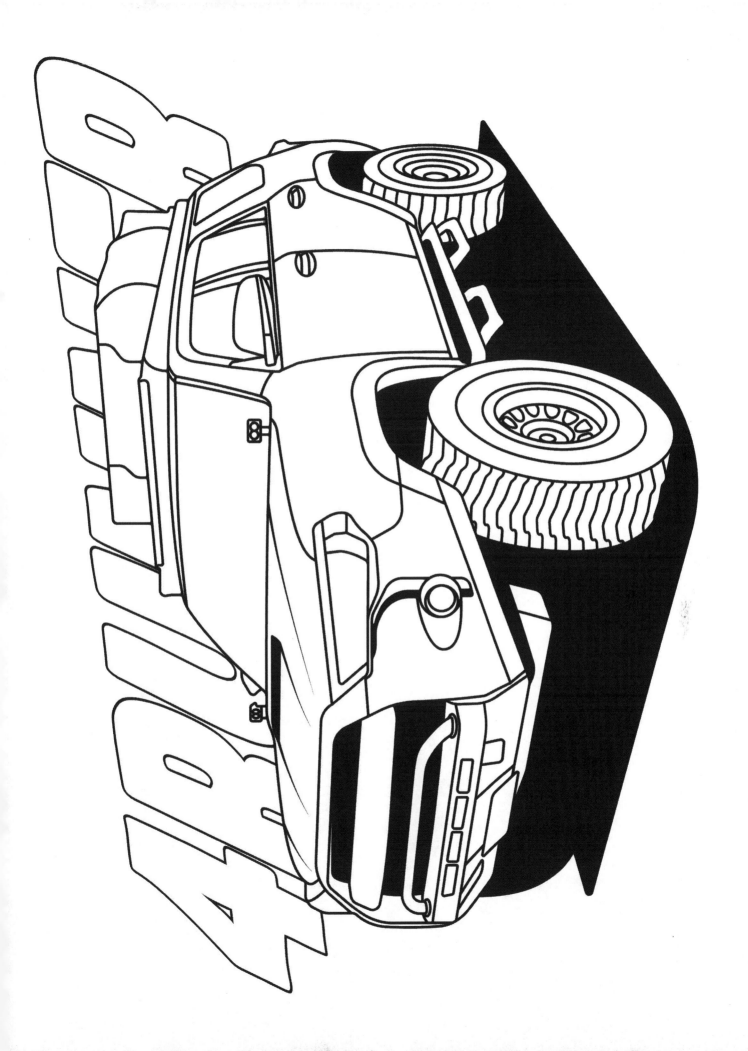

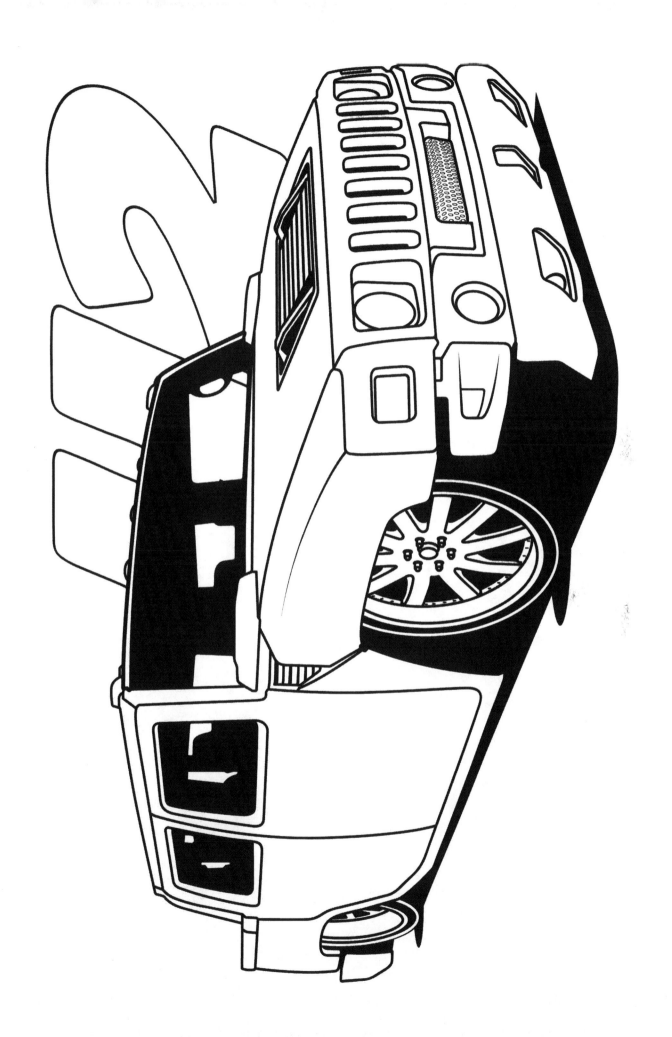

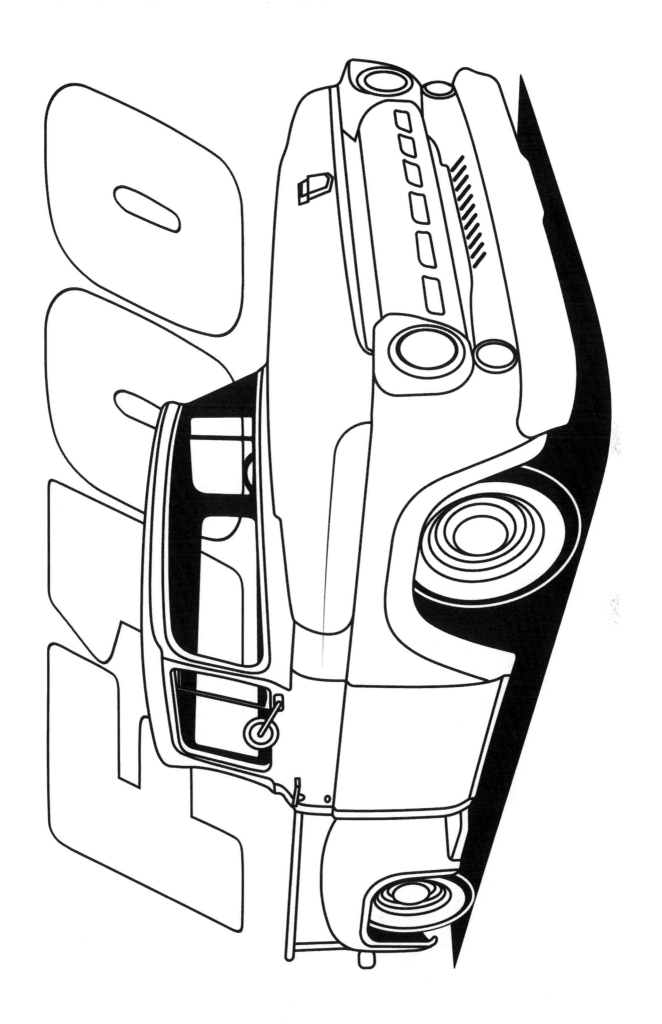

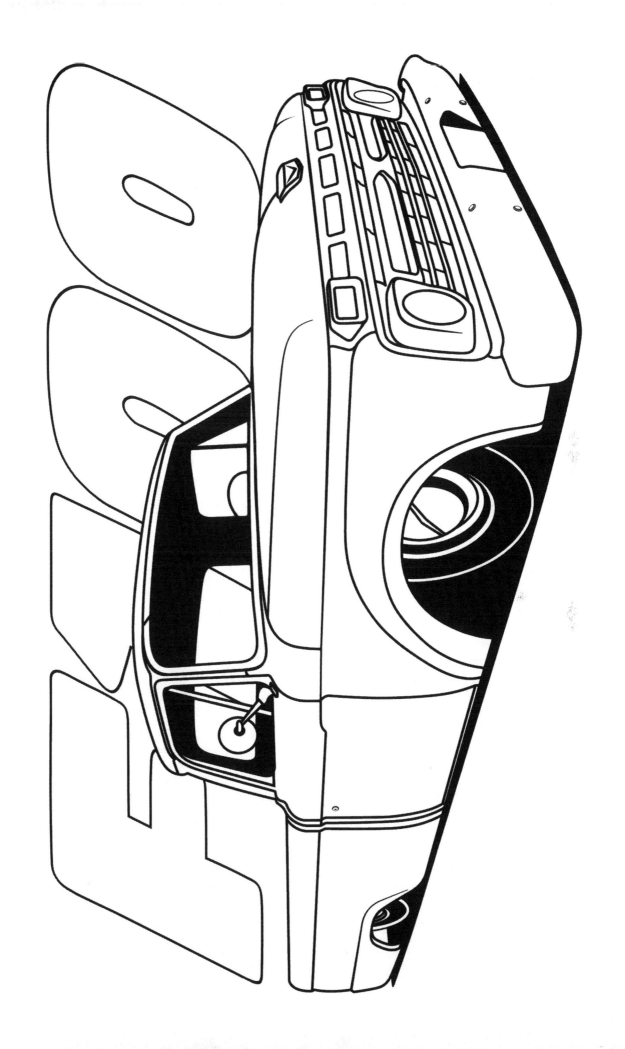

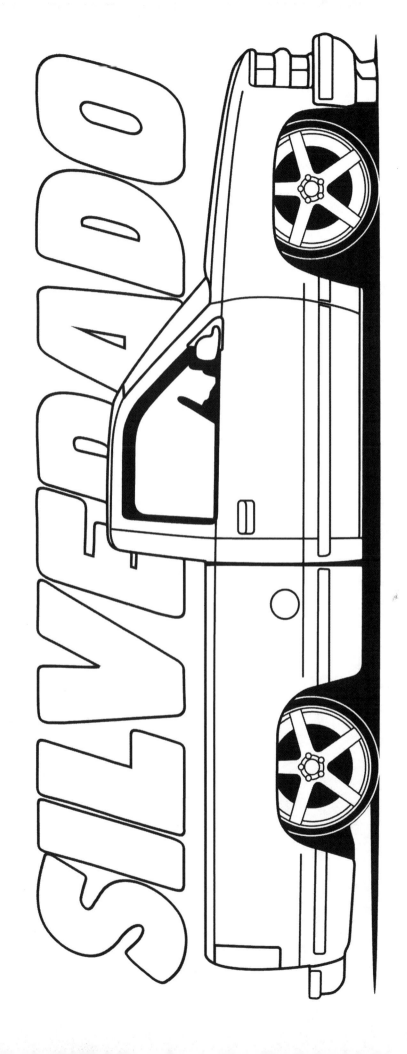

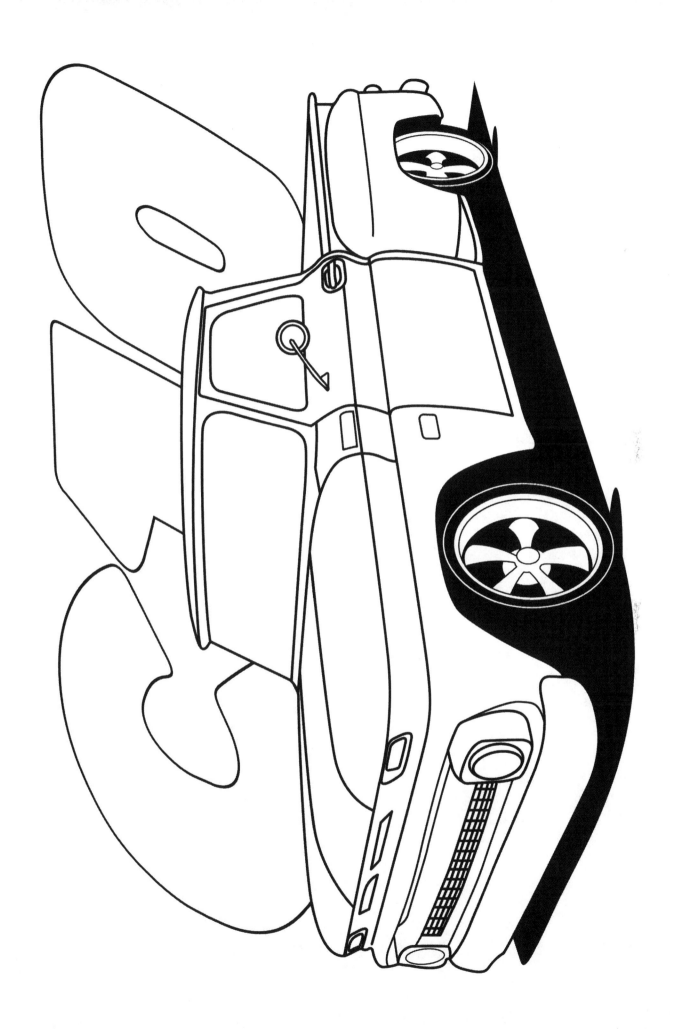

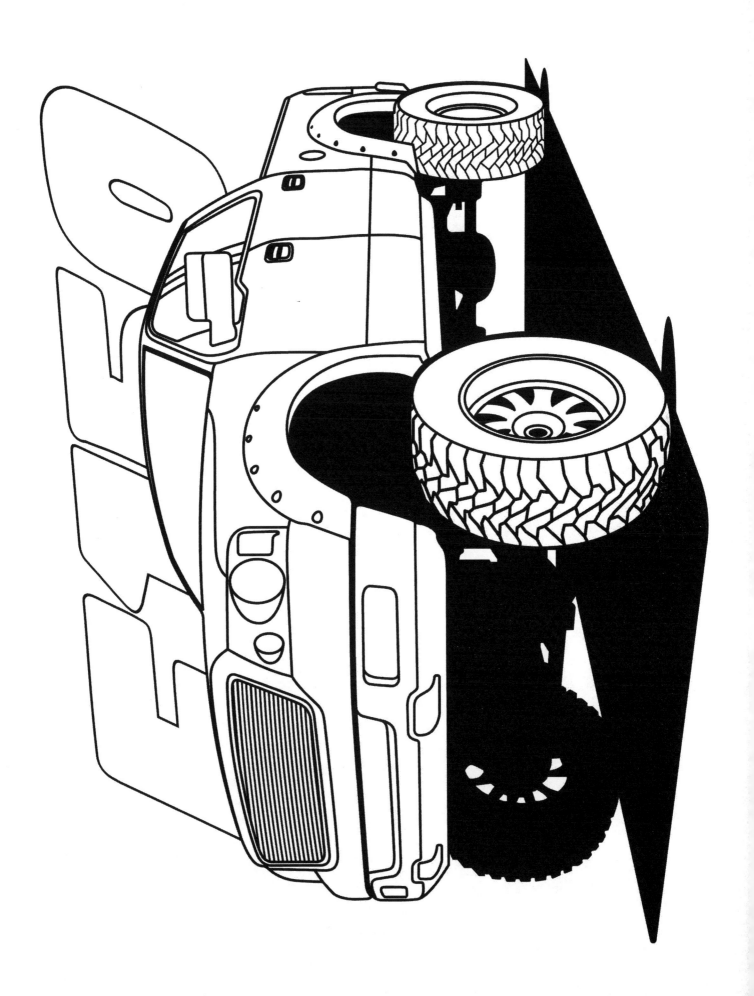

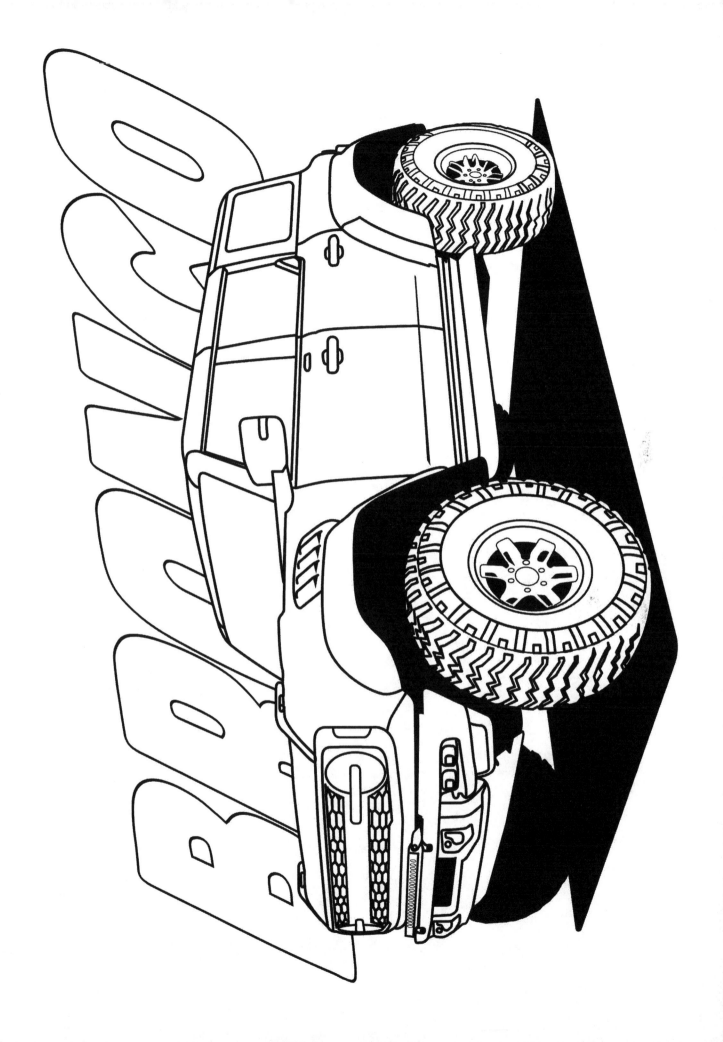

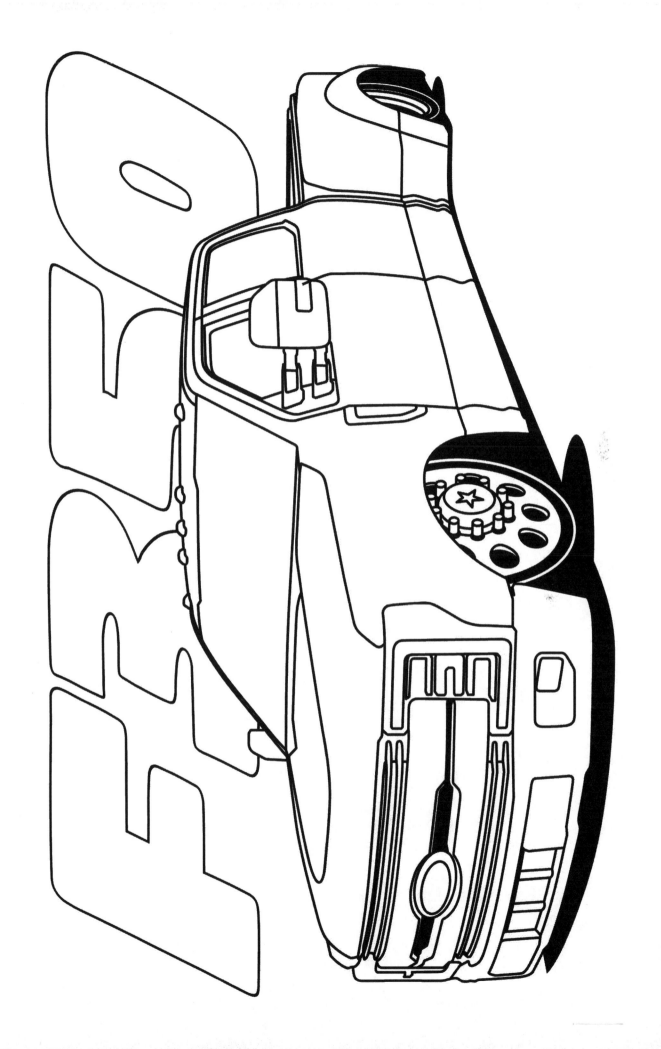

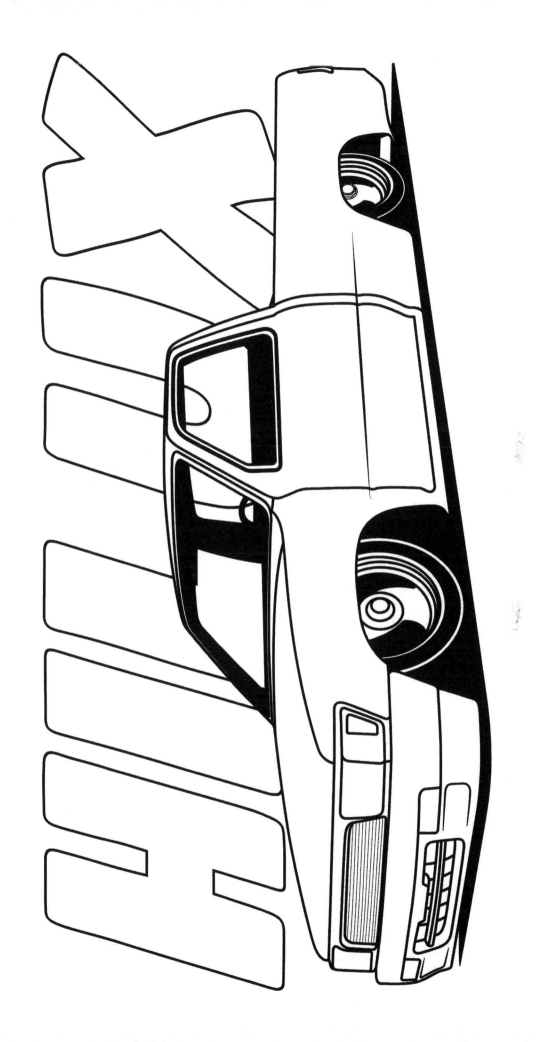

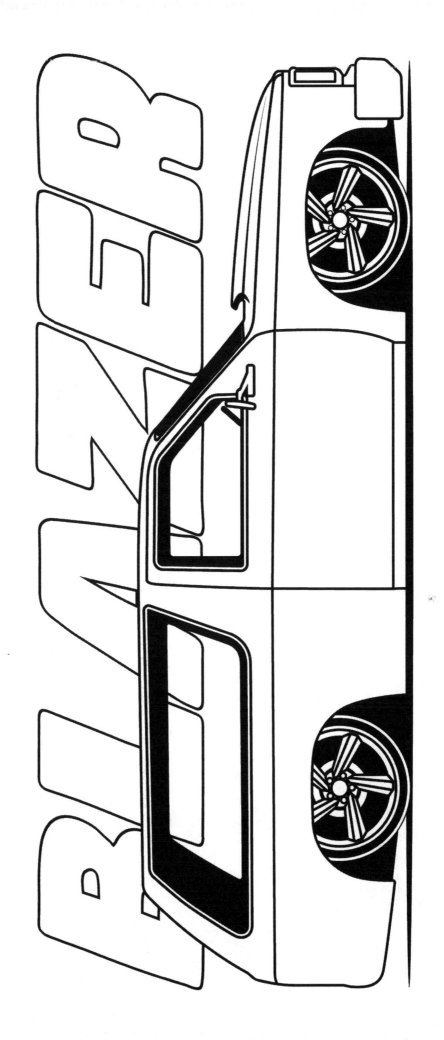

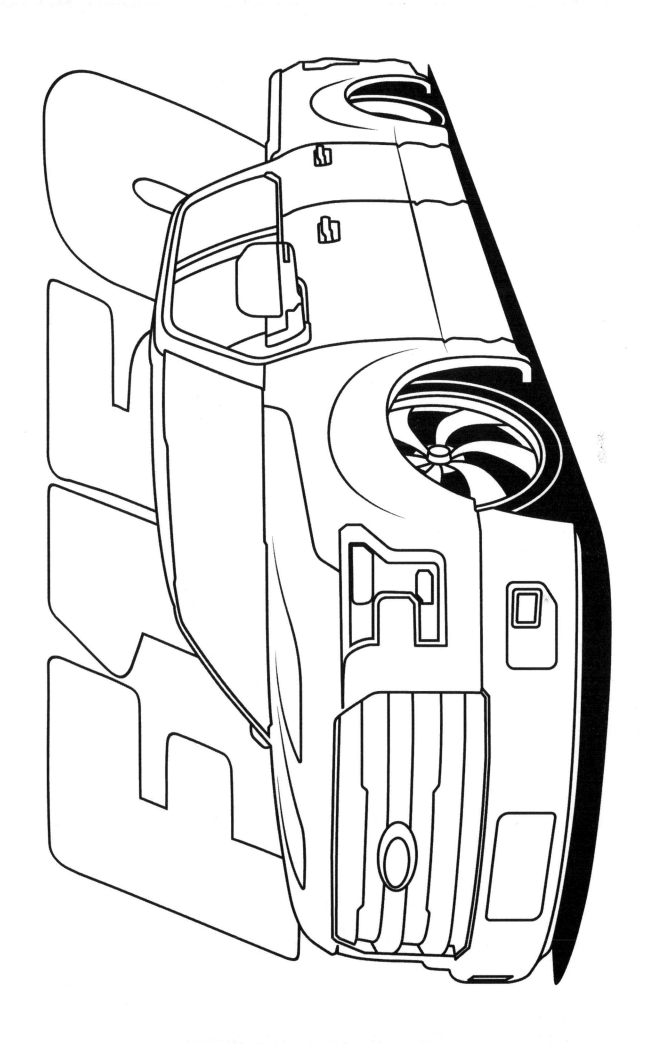

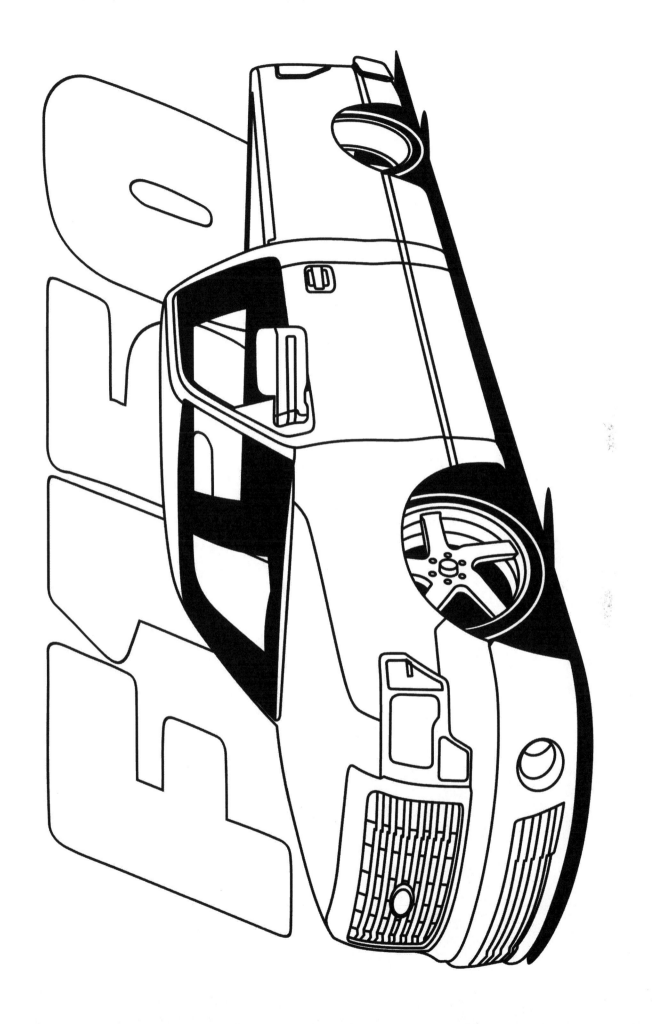

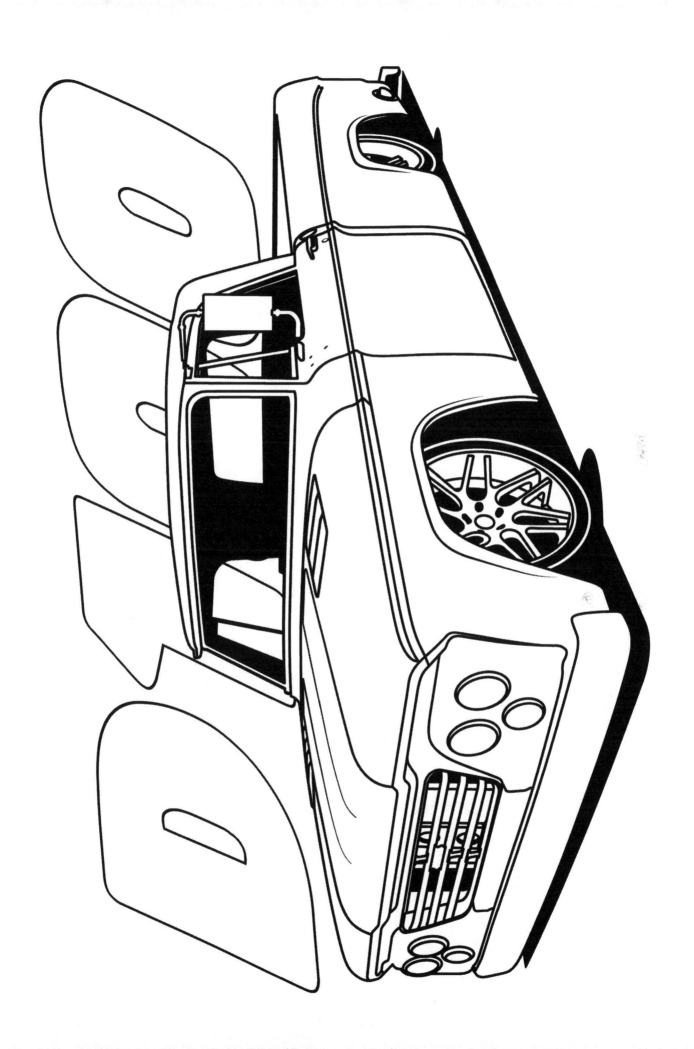

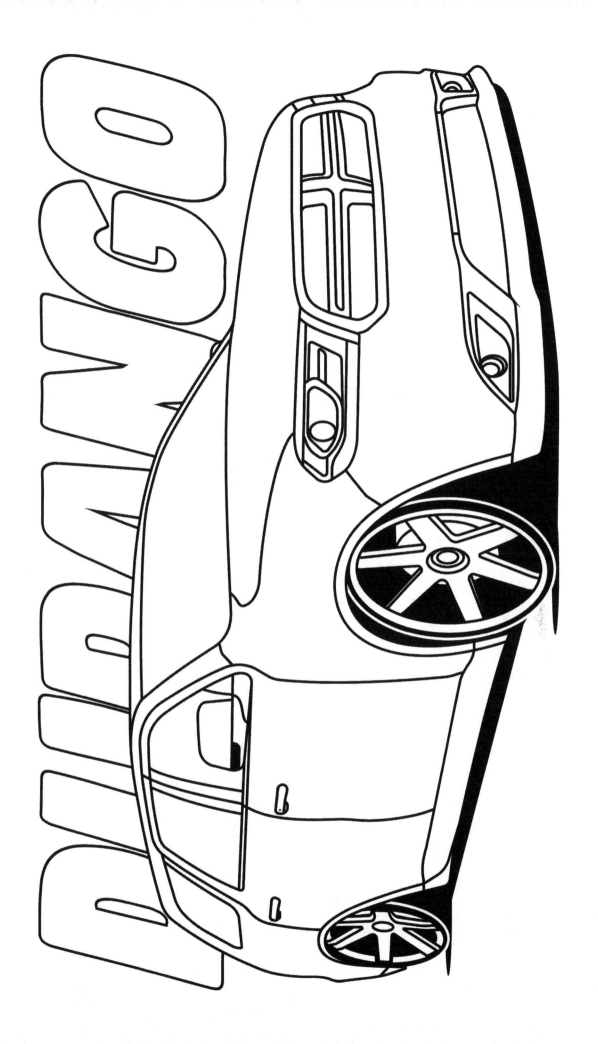

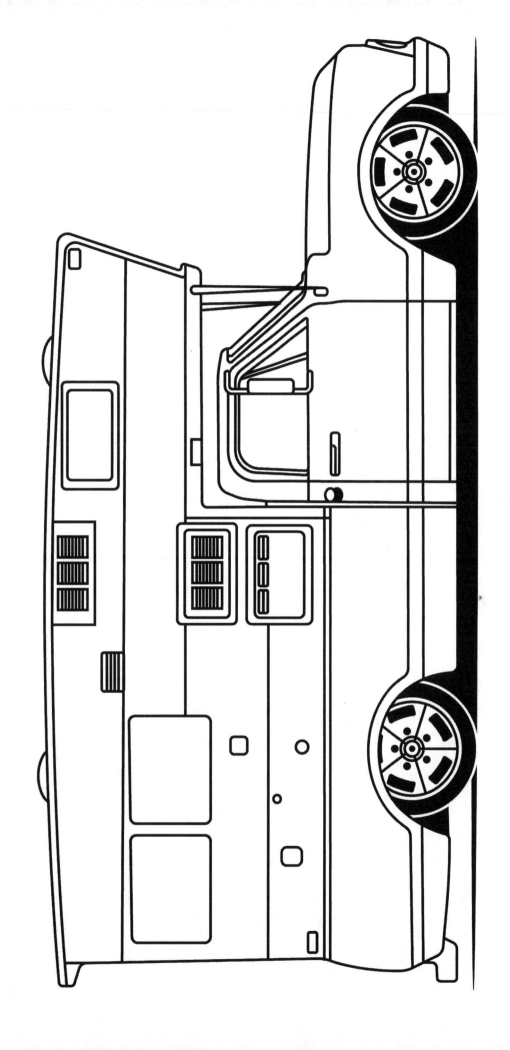

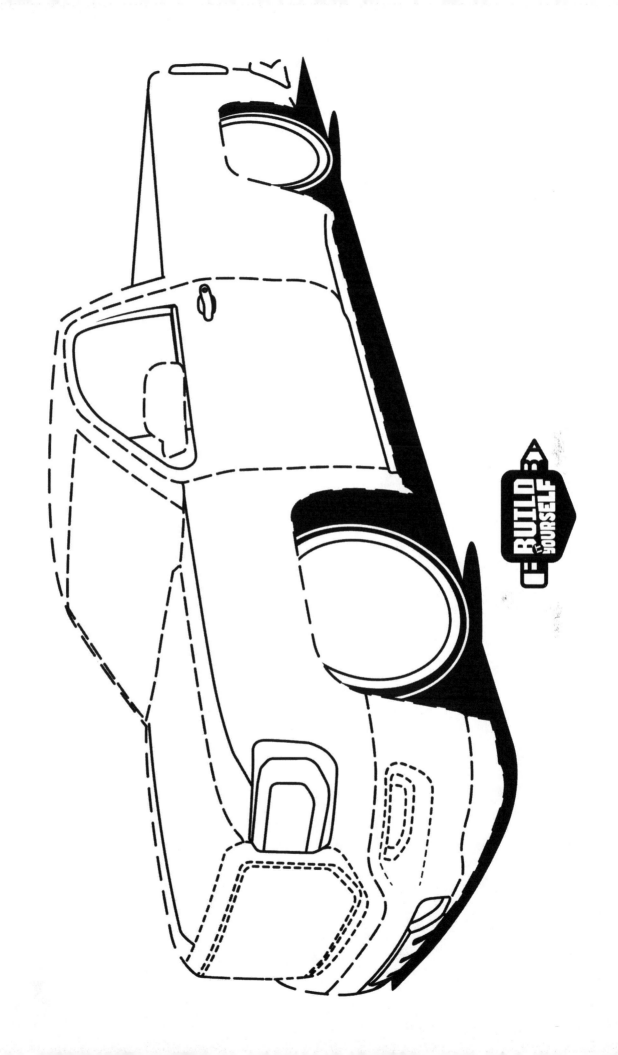

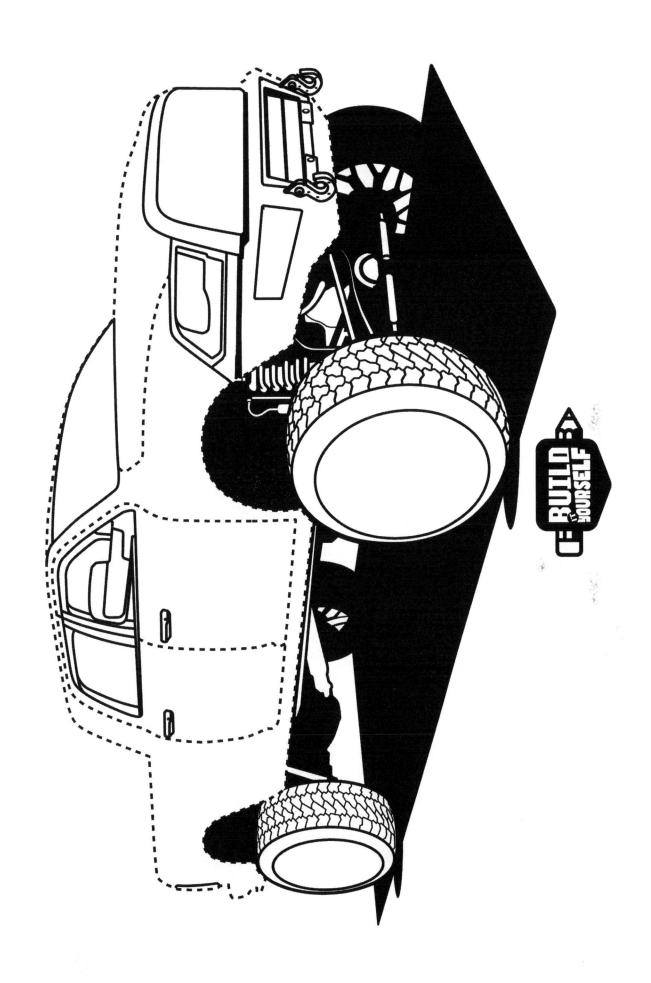

WWW.HEYDANIELVERA.COM